ADVENTURE TALES OF
BENJAMIN BANNEKER

ADVENTURE TALES OF
BENJAMIN BANNEKER

From The Book

ADVENTURE TALES OF AMERICA
An Illustrated History Of The United States, 1492-1877

Jody Potts, Ph.D.

ILLUSTRATORS
Foy Lisenby, Ph.D.
Jerry D. Poole, Ph.D.

Signal Media Publishers

Dallas, Texas

AUTHOR

Jody Potts, a native Texan, has taught graduate courses in American intellectual, cultural, and political history at Southern Methodist University in Dallas for two decades and served as visiting professor at Alaska Pacific University for three summers. In SMU's Master of Liberal Arts Program she currently teaches a course on the history of American ideas, **Ideas that Shaped the American Character,** and a course she originated, **The Lively Mind: Creative and Critical Thinking Using Both Sides of the Brain.** She holds a B.S. degree in education from Baylor University, an M.A. degree in history from Southern Methodist University, and a Ph.D. degree in history from the University of North Texas.

A specialist in left and right brain learning techniques, Dr. Potts pioneered the integration of these techniques with the teaching and writing of history. In 1993 she wrote *Adventure Tales of America: An Illustrated History of the United States, 1492-1877,* an innovative book that accelerates learning by simultaneously giving information to the left brain through words, analysis, and structure and the right brain through pictures, humor, and drama. *Adventure Tales of America,* now a multimedia program, has raised state history scores throughout the country, as much as eighteen percent with grade-level students and 115 percent with at-risk students.

Adventure Tales of Benjamin Banneker is an expansion of Banneker's story that appears in *Adventure Tales of America: An Illustrated History of the United States, 1492-1877.* (shown opposite)

In 1984 Dr. Potts founded **The Lively Mind,** a national consulting firm offering seminars in left and right brain learning techniques for students, faculties, and administrators. Participating groups have included public schools nationwide, state social studies councils, the Council for Support and Advancement of Education, and the University of Texas at Austin senior faculty.

ILLUSTRATORS

Foy Lisenby, a specialist in American social and cultural history and a gifted cartoonist, served fifteen years as chairman of the University of Central Arkansas History Department. He has published numerous articles and, in 1996, a biography of Charles Hillman Brough.

Jerry D. Poole served as professor of art at the University of Central Arkansas until 1989, chairing the Art Department for seventeen years. He currently is Artist-in-Residence and a consultant for the Center for Academic Excellence at UCA. He is an accomplished silhouette artist and specializes in watercolor painting.

PUBLISHER

Copyright © 2000 by Signal Media Publishers
SignalMedia Publishers acknowledges the use of some of its previously copyrighted materials from *Adventure Tales of America: An Illustrated History of the United States, 1492-1877.*

Location photography by Jody Potts.

Signal Media Publishers specializes in innovative learning materials.
To preview and order visit **www.adventuretales.com** or call 1-800-494-2445.

ISBN: 1-887337-07-5   Library of Congress Card Number: 00-191623   Printed in the United States of America   10 9 8 7 6 5 4 3 2 1

Adventure Tales of America

Multimedia U.S. History Program

Get set for an adventure in learning!

For more information go to

www.adventuretales.com

or call 1-800-494-2445.

ACKNOWLEDGMENTS

The Maryland Historical Society in Baltimore holds important Benjamin Banneker sources, including Banneker's journal, almanacs, and letters. I would like to thank Mary Herbert, Assistant Curator of Manuscripts at the Maryland Historical Society, for her help in making these and other sources available for my research.

The Benjamin Banneker Historical Park and Museum in Oella, Maryland, marks the site of Banneker's 100-acre farm. The Baltimore County Department of Recreation and Parks funded the archeological projects that determined the exact location of Banneker's cabin.

Oella is one mile from Ellicott City and ten miles from Baltimore.

I am grateful to Steven Lee, Historian/Park and Museum Director, for his extensive knowledge of Banneker which he so generously shared on a tour of the museum and Banneker cabin site.

The Howard County Visitors' Center staff welcomed me to Ellicott City and helped me understand the social, cultural, intellectual, and economic atmosphere of Banneker's community. I appreciate their insight and hospitality.

Jody Potts

★

Contents

1731   1806

Benjamin Banneker was a free African-American who reflected the 18th century spirit of scientific inquiry. He became a respected mathematician and astronomer.

Benjamin Banneker was born in 1731 near Baltimore, Maryland. He lived until 1806.

He made his living farming.

He made his life an adventure in learning.

Fascinated with timepieces, at age 22 he made a clock carved entirely from wood.

A gifted mathematician, in his late fifties, he became a self-taught surveyor and astronomer.

He was appointed by President George Washington to the surveying team that laid the boundaries and streets of Washington, D.C., in 1791.

Intrigued with astronomy, he published the first Maryland almanac (from 1792 to 1797), doing all the scientific computations himself.

From childhood Benjamin Banneker had an active life of the mind, and he never stopped learning. Read on for his exciting story.

GRANDMOTHER MOLLY

Benjamin Banneker had an English and African heritage. Molly Welsh, Benjamin's white, English grandmother, came from England to Maryland as an indentured servant in 1683. Why did she come?

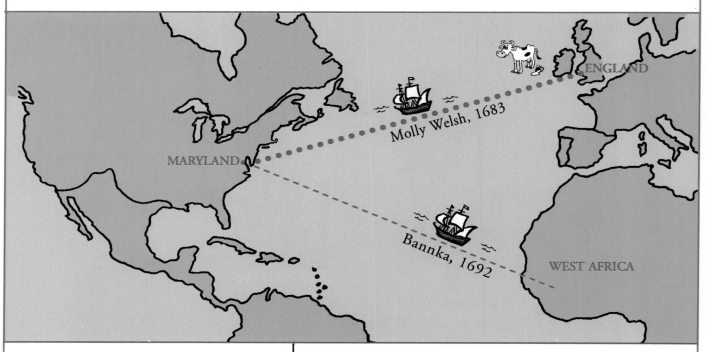

ENGLAND

Molly Welsh, 1683

MARYLAND

Bannka, 1692

WEST AFRICA

IT ALL STARTED WITH SPILLED MILK.

Molly had been a milkmaid on an English farm. One day a cow she was milking kicked over the pail of milk. Molly's employer had her arrested.

LUCKILY, MOLLY COULD READ.

An English law reduced punishment for prisoners if they proved they could read, allowing them to go to America as **indentured servants** (persons who exchanged seven years of unpaid work for passage to America). Molly called for a Bible, read from it, and sailed to America.

1680   1683   1690   1692   1696   1700

Molly worked seven years as an indentured servant for a Maryland tobacco farmer. In 1690 she gained her freedom and purchased land near the Patapsco River in Baltimore County.
In 1692 she bought an African-born slave named <u>Bannka</u>, later called <u>Banneky</u>, to help her farm the land.

Banneky was the son of a Wolof kingdom tribal chief in Senegal, near the west coast of Africa. He had been captured, enslaved, and sent to Maryland to be sold. He and Molly spoke different languages, but they gradually learned to communicate and became friends.

Molly opposed slavery and soon freed Banneky. About 1696 she married him, at the risk of her own freedom. A 1684 Maryland law had declared marriage between whites and blacks illegal.

Molly adopted Banneky's name and his people, and they withdrew from white society. Banneky died at a young age, leaving Molly with four daughters. Mary was the oldest.

PARENTS: MARY AND ROBERT BANNEKY

In 1730 Molly's daughter Mary married a freed black slave
named Robert, an African from Guinea.

British-American
Colonies, 1700s

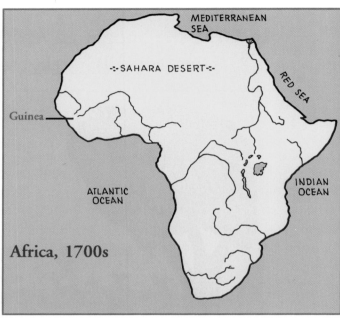

Africa, 1700s

Robert had been captured and enslaved in Guinea about 1720. He was brought to
Maryland and sold to a tobacco farmer who lived near Molly Welsh. A proud,
dignified man, he resisted enslavement by escaping but was recaptured.

Fortunately, a kind land owner bought Robert and
sometime before 1730 granted him his freedom.
Robert had become a Christian, and at the time of his
baptism into the Anglican church he received both his
freedom and his name, Robert. He had no last name.

Mary and Robert married in 1730 and used
her last name, **Banneky,** later changing it to
Banneker. They lived with Molly Welsh and helped
her farm until they could save enough to buy their
own land. Soon Mary and Robert started their family.

Benjamin Banneker was born November 9, 1731. Then
came four daughters, including Jemima, Minta, and Molly.
(The records do not tell us the oldest daughter's name.) Benjamin
and his sisters had a great legacy from their grandparents and parents: freedom.

Molly Welsh		Bannka (Banneky)
	married 1696	
Mary Banneky (Banneker)		Robert
	married 1730	
	Benjamin Banneker	

1731   1737   1759   1806

In the 1730s most African-Americans in Maryland were slaves.

The few blacks who were free were not always sure they could keep their freedom. Robert and Mary Banneker decided that owning land would make their freedom more secure, so they worked hard and saved their money to buy a 25-acre farm.

In 1737 Robert bought a large, second farm, 100 acres near the Patapsco River falls–a big achievement for a former slave born in Africa.

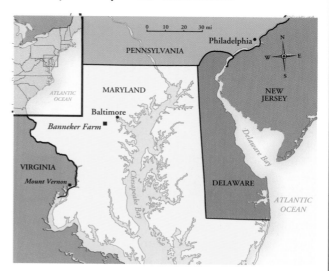

The farm, near that of Grandmother Molly, was ten miles from Baltimore, Maryland, and within 100 miles of Mount Vernon, the future home of George Washington. The lives of Benjamin Banneker and George Washington (who lived from 1732 to 1799) would connect in 1791.

Robert made six-year old Benjamin a joint owner of the new farm because he feared that when he died, Maryland laws might keep Benjamin from inheriting the farm.

When Robert died in 1759, Benjamin, age 28, became sole owner of the land.

Benjamin spent his life farming the land. He never married but enjoyed family life among his nearby relatives.

According to his cousin John Herndon, Benjamin was a favorite of Grandmother Molly and enjoyed many years of companionship with her.

Grandmother Molly taught Benjamin to read and write from her only book, the Bible. She took pleasure in his learning.

And she told him stories about his Grandfather Banneky—whom Martha Tyson,* a family acquaintance, described as "a man of industry, integrity, fine disposition and dignified manners."

(*In 1836 Martha Ellicott Tyson wrote *A Sketch of the Life of Benjamin Banneker; From Notes Taken in 1836.* Based on interviews with Banneker's acquaintances and relatives, it is one of the most important original sources on Banneker.)

Benjamin attended a one-room Quaker school for four winters, along with several white students and another free black, Jacob Hall.

A gifted student, Benjamin liked to invent math puzzles. According to Jacob, Benjamin's delight was to "dive into his books." (Tyson, *A Sketch*)

1731   1751   1806

In 1751, at age 20, Benjamin Banneker began a venture that revealed astonishing mathematical and mechanical ability.

He borrowed a pocket watch for a week to see how it worked.

He decided he could create his own timepiece. After taking the watch apart, he drew the pieces and memorized how they fit together.

Guided only by his drawings and working for two years, Banneker made a clock by carving the parts from wood.

The clock kept perfect time (striking every hour) for more than 50 years.

Throughout his life people came from miles around to see this unusual clock made of wood— and the remarkable man who made it.

1731   1772   1806

In 1772 five Quaker brothers named Ellicott migrated from Pennsylvania to Maryland and started a new community, Ellicott Mills. Later renamed Ellicott City, it was nine miles from Baltimore and one mile from Banneker's farm.

The Ellicott brothers–Joseph, Andrew III, Nathaniel, Thomas, and John–had been successful millers in Pennsylvania. With an entrepreneurial spirit, they brought their families to Maryland seeking an ideal spot for a new gristmill to grind wheat into flour.

They decided to settle near Baltimore because of its growing importance as a commercial port on Chesapeake Bay.

They bought land near the Patapsco River in the middle of Maryland's tobacco country.

"Tobacco country is hardly an ideal spot for a wheat-grinding business," their neighbors observed.

But the Ellicotts knew good wheat country when they saw it. They transformed the economy by convincing neighboring farmers to grow wheat instead of tobacco.

Farmers who did so made money. As they grew more prosperous, a new town called Ellicott City began to develop.

Banneker lived in a sparsely settled area of Maryland. With the coming of the Ellicotts, his world had grown, and so would his friendships.

Banneker made frequent trips to observe the Ellicotts' new gristmill. He watched it grind wheat into flour and corn into meal.

He was even more interested in the mill's machinery and tried to figure out how it worked.

He also enjoyed visiting with neighbors at the store the Ellicotts built (shown below, second building from the left with its second-story porch). He entertained them with math puzzles and talked with them about the weather, crops, and news of the day.

This picture and the one below are from a lithograph by E. Sachse & Co., Baltimore, 1854. Courtesy of Maryland Historical Society.

George Ellicott (son of Andrew III) expanded Banneker's intellectual horizons. The two men became friends when Banneker was forty-seven and Ellicott was eighteen.

George, one of the best mathematicians and amateur astronomers of his time, liked to share his knowledge. He gave free lectures and demonstrations with his telescope to interested neighbors, including Banneker, who gathered at his home (shown at left). He occasionally visited Banneker in his cabin and was impressed with Banneker's clock.

1731   1789   1806

At age 58, Banneker found a new direction for his life: astronomy.

In 1789 George Ellicott, Banneker's Quaker friend and neighbor, loaned Banneker some surveying and astronomy textbooks, along with a telescope and an oval, drop-leaf table.

By 1790 Benjamin mastered the content of the surveying and astronomy books.

A year later he astounded George Ellicott by calculating a 1791 ephemeris.

AMANING!

An ephemeris is a set of astronomical projections of tides, eclipses, sunrises, and sunsets for the calendar year. It is the basic information for an almanac.

1731   1790   1806

Eager to increase his knowledge of astronomy, Banneker found a way to retire from farming and devote himself to science. About 1790 he sold his farm to the Ellicott family, reserving the right to live there the rest of his life.

Freed from having to make a living on his farm, Banneker slept during the day and studied the stars by night. He noted his observations in a journal, creating an ephemeris for each month of the year.

Banneker's journal entry below records the last page of September and the first page of October, 1795. The journal includes monthly records for several years.

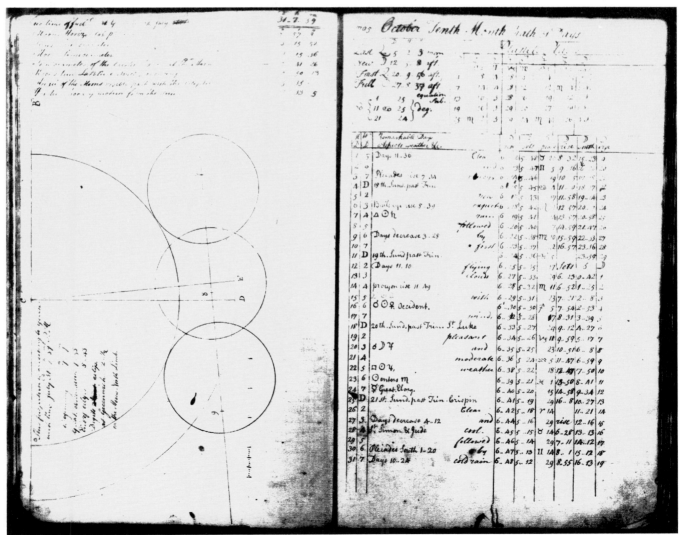

From Benjamin Banneker's Journal, Courtesy of Maryland Historical Society.

1731   1791   1806

In 1791 Banneker sent his ephemeris to the surveyor Andrew Ellicott (Joseph Ellicott's son) and received the surprise of his life!

President George Washington had appointed Andrew Ellicott to survey the site chosen for the nation's new capital, at first called Territory of Columbia and later named Washington, District of Columbia (D.C.).

Washington, at the request of Congress, had chosen the site himself. It was about fifteen miles north of his home, Mount Vernon.

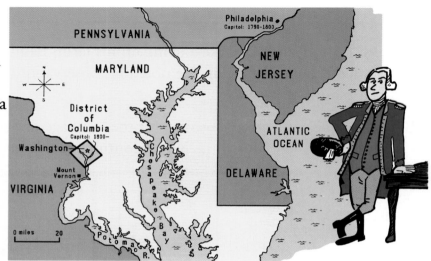

Andrew Ellicott needed an assistant. He was impressed by Banneker's astronomical expertise (essential for surveying land) and recommended him for the survey team to Thomas Jefferson, who was in charge of the project. Then at Jefferson's recommendation, Washington confirmed Banneker's appointment.

1731   1791   1806

From February to April 1791, Banneker assisted Ellicott in surveying the ten-mile square capital and its federal city named for George Washington. Pierre L'Enfant used Ellicott's survey to map the city.

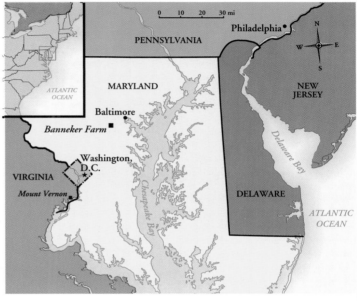

At night Benjamin Banneker observed the stars from a hole in the observatory tent. He then used their lattitude and longitude to compute base points for the capital's streets.

1731   1791   1806

On March 28, 1791, President George Washington came to visit the capital site.

There is no evidence that Banneker met the president. However, Benjamin must have been proud as Washington reviewed the team's work.

Washington, himself a surveyor, had as a young man of 19 laid out the city of Alexandria, just west of the Potomac River.

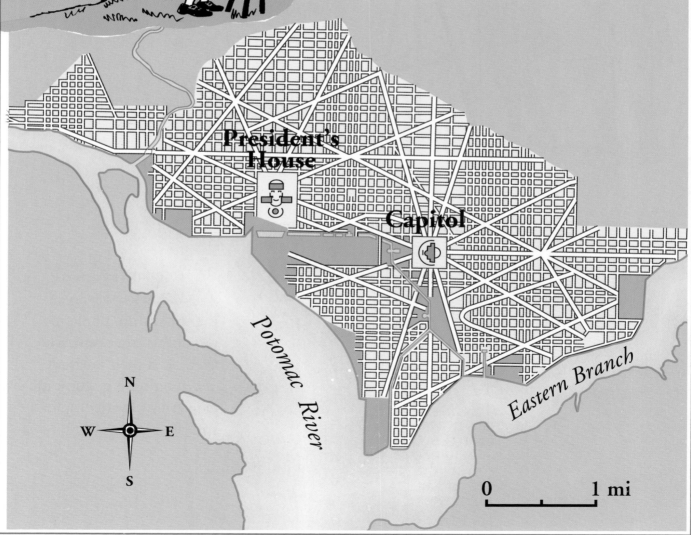

Today Washington, D.C. is one of the most beautiful capitals in the world. Although Banneker would not recognize the buildings, he would certainly know his way around town.

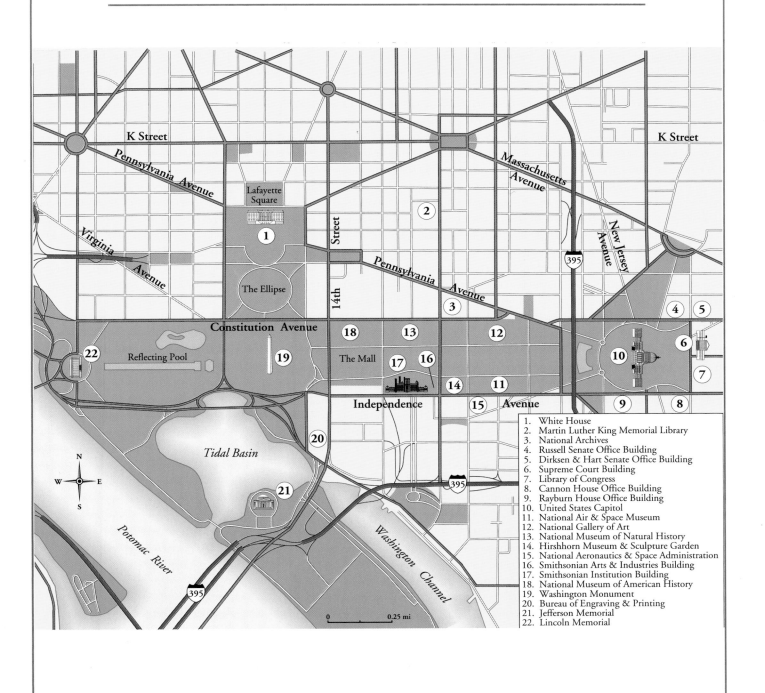

1. White House
2. Martin Luther King Memorial Library
3. National Archives
4. Russell Senate Office Building
5. Dirksen & Hart Senate Office Building
6. Supreme Court Building
7. Library of Congress
8. Cannon House Office Building
9. Rayburn House Office Building
10. United States Capitol
11. National Air & Space Museum
12. National Gallery of Art
13. National Museum of Natural History
14. Hirshhorn Museum & Sculpture Garden
15. National Aeronautics & Space Administration
16. Smithsonian Arts & Industries Building
17. Smithsonian Institution Building
18. National Museum of American History
19. Washington Monument
20. Bureau of Engraving & Printing
21. Jefferson Memorial
22. Lincoln Memorial

1792—Upon returning home from surveying the capital, Banneker fulfilled his ambition to write *Benjamin Banneker's Almanac.*

Unlike Benjamin Franklin in *Poor Richard's Almanac,* Banneker did his own computing of the tides, eclipses, sunrises, and sunsets.

But like Franklin, he included proverbs and essays to entertain and instruct.

Among the essays were several on antislavery, written by members of the Maryland Society for the Abolition of Slavery.

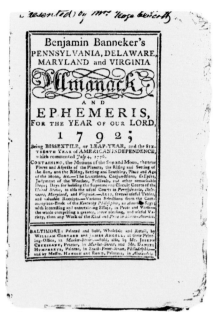

Courtesy of Maryland Historical Society.

Banneker's publisher asked Dr. David Rittenhouse of Philadelphia to review the almanac before its printing. Rittenhouse, the country's foremost scientist and Benjamin Franklin's successor as president of the American Philosophical Society, reported:

Banneker's almanac was a big success. He published one annually for six years. By 1797 twenty-eight editions had been printed.

1731   1776   1783   1806

During the Revolutionary War many farmers grew wheat for American soldiers. Banneker may have been among them.

Banneker must have read with puzzlement Thomas Jefferson's words in the Declaration of Independence because in 1791 he would write Jefferson with questions about them.

1731	1791-93	1806

Banneker's 1793 almanac contained an exchange of letters with Thomas Jefferson.

In 1791 Banneker sent a letter and a copy of his first almanac to Secretary of State Thomas Jefferson, author of the Declaration of Independence.

August 19, 1791

Sir...I suppose it is a truth too well attested to you...that we are a race of Beings who have long laboured under the abuse and censure of the world, that we have long been looked upon with an eye of contempt, and that we have long been considered rather as brutish than human, and scarcely capable of mental endowments.

Sir, I hope I may safely admit...that you are friendly and well disposed towards us...willing and ready to lend your aid....

Sir, suffer me to recall...that time in which the arms and tyranny of the British Crown were exerted...to reduce you to a state of servitude....This, Sir, was a time in which you clearly saw into the injustice of...slavery...and held forth this true and invaluable doctrine: "We hold these truths to be self evident, that all men are created equal, and that they are endowed by their creator with certain inalienable rights, that amongst these are life, liberty, and the pursuit of happiness."

...but Sir, how pitiable it is to reflect, that...you should at the same time counteract [God's] mercies, in detaining through fraud and violence my brethren under groaning captivity and cruel oppression....

...as Job proposed to his friends, "Put your souls in their souls' stead...and thus shall you need neither the direction of myself or others in what manner to proceed herein...."

And now, Sir, I shall conclude and subscribe my self with the most profound respect.

Your most obedient humble servant,
Benjamin Banneker

1731   1791   1806

Soon after receiving Banneker's letter, Jefferson replied.

August 30, 1791

Sir, I thank you sincerely for your letter of the 19th...and for the Almanac....Nobody wishes more than I do to see such proofs as you exhibit, that nature has given to our black brethren, talents equal to those of the other colors of men, and that the appearance of a want of them is owing merely to the degraded condition of their existence, both in Africa and America.

I can add with truth, that nobody wishes more ardently to see a good system commenced for raising the condition both of their body and mind to what it ought to be, as fast as the imbecility of their present existence, and other circumstances which cannot be neglected, will admit.

I have taken the liberty of sending your Almanac to Monsieur de Condorcet, Secretary of the Academy of Sciences at Paris...because I considered it as a document to which your whole colour had a right for their justification against the doubts which have been entertained of them.

I am with great esteem, Sir, your most obedient humble servant.
Thomas Jefferson

1731   1806

<hr>

Banneker spent his last years observing nature and playing his flute and violin under a favorite pear tree.

<hr>

Banneker belonged to no church, although he dressed as a Quaker and often attended the Society of Friends Meeting House.

Martha Ellicott Tyson, daughter of George Ellicott, said, "His life was one of constant worship in the great temples of nature." (Tyson, *A Sketch*)

1731   1806

In 1806 Benjamin Banneker died at age 74.
Through words, work, and intellect he demonstrated that with freedom to learn, intellectual accomplishments are no respecter of race.

An obituary in the *Federal Gazette* described Banneker as "well known among scientific men as an astronomer and mathematician."

His reputation as an African-American intellectual widened after his death. In 1836 Martha Ellicott Tyson wrote *A Sketch* of Banneker's life. Other memoirs followed.

In 1852 Banneker's manuscripts, letters, and almanacs were given to the Maryland Historical Society.

In 1870 Frederick Douglass, the noted African-American abolitionist, said:

> "We as a people are especially in need of just such examples of mental industry and success as I believe the life of Benjamin Banneker furnish."

1731   1854   2031

1854—In honor of Benjamin Banneker, African-American men in Philadelphia who formed the Young Men's Mutual Instruction Society named it the Banneker Institute.

1731   1998   2031

Today the Benjamin Banneker Historical Park and Museum, built in 1998 by the Baltimore County Department of Recreation and Parks, marks the site of Banneker's farm.

In 1985, at the request of local historians, Baltimore County bought land that had been Benjamin Banneker's farmstead. Supporters formed Friends of Benjamin Banneker Historical Park to spearhead the 142-acre historical development. The Benjamin Banneker Historical Park and Museum was dedicated in 1998. Through research, exhibits, and educational programs, it continues the discovery and presentation of Benjamin Banneker's remarkable life.

Archaeologists have discovered the foundation of Banneker's cabin
on this site in the Banneker Historical Park.
The Banneker Museum displays many
artifacts also found here.

Dismayed that boys often stole fruit from his orchards, Banneker said,
"I have no influence with the rising generation."
History proves him shortsighted.

To experience the life of Benjamin Banneker first-hand, visit the 142-acre Benjamin Banneker Historical Park and Museum at 300 Oella Avenue, Oella, Maryland.

Historical exhibits and nature trails will inform and delight you. Benjamin Banneker's life will inspire you.

INDEX